BREAD FOR OUR JOURNEY
Walking With Jesus Each Day

Jeff Smith

This book is dedicated to
my father,
Donald E. Smith

BREAD FOR OUR JOURNEY

Walking With Jesus Each Day

The Word Among Us

9639 Doctor Perry Road

Ijamsville, Maryland 21754

ISBN: 0-932085-17-2

© 1998 by The Word Among Us Press

All rights reserved.

Cover design by David Crosson

No part of this publication may be reproduced, stored in a retrieval system, or transmitted in any form or by any means—electronic, mechanical, photocopy, recording, or any other— except for brief quotations in printed reviews, without the prior permission of the publisher.

Made and printed in the United States of America.

The author wishes to thank Dr. André Leyva for his contributions to this book.

Contents

Introduction
6

Welcome Holy Spirit
9

I Will Never Leave You
21

God Is Truly In Our Hearts
31

Bread for Our Journey
33

One With the Lord
43

Jesus, Bread From Heaven
45

Introduction

Because most of us have experienced family life, we can understand to some degree what it means to have a relationship with God, our heavenly Father, and with his Son, Jesus. The Holy Spirit, however, often seems hidden from us. God wants to give us the opportunity to experience his Spirit in a powerful and vibrant way. We can welcome him into our lives, into our families, and into our whole world.

The promise given by the Father at Pentecost is that we can stay close to the Holy Spirit who has been poured into our hearts (Romans 5:5). As we listen to the Spirit, we will find him leading us into a deeper relationship, both with Jesus and with God our Father. Scripture tells us that the Spirit within us cries out: "Abba, Father" (Romans 8:15) and that the Spirit has come to teach us about the majesty and the glory of Jesus (John 16:13-14).

The Holy Spirit wants to manifest God's presence

to us throughout our days. In this book, *Bread for Our Journey*, we look at the Spirit's work of drawing us into God's presence and transforming us by his love. He can become a part of our everyday lives. Thanks to the Spirit, we can experience God in so many different ways. We can hear his voice in scripture; he can speak to our hearts as we pray. The Spirit feeds us as we receive Jesus' life and love in the Eucharist. He is even with us in the day-to-day situations of our lives. In all of these ways, we can be confident that the Holy Spirit is at work, moving us to love Jesus and our Father more deeply.

Jesus taught his disciples to pray for the Holy Spirit boldly and persistently: "If you . . . know how to give good gifts to your children, how much more will the heavenly Father give the Holy Spirit to those who ask him" (Luke 11:13). Let us pray: "Come, Holy Spirit, and renew the face of the earth."

Jeff Smith
The Word Among Us

Welcome Holy Spirit

The Holy Spirit extends an invitation to all of God's children. He wants us to welcome him into our hearts and into our world. He wants us to experience him as the very presence of God in our midst. As we recount how the Spirit brought life to the early church on that first Pentecost (Acts 2:1-4), we call on that same Spirit to renew us today with the same power and joy that filled those early disciples.

In *Bread for Our Journey*, we want to welcome the Holy Spirit as he continues to descend on God's children. We will consider how the Spirit is alive and active in so many ways—and how we have the opportunity to know God's presence every day of our lives. While this chapter recounts the first Pentecost, subsequent chapters consider how God is present in our midst today. He dwells in our hearts, longing to speak to us. He meets us in the Eucharist. He is present when we gather together in Jesus' name. He speaks to us through scripture. He comes to us in the poor and needy.

Every day, the Holy Spirit is waiting for us to call upon him. We can learn to invite him to be present with us and to sanctify every moment, every conversation, every joyful happening as well as every trying circumstance. In the Holy Spirit, Jesus' promise rings true: "I will not leave you desolate" (John 14:18).

"A little while, and you will see me no more." (John 16:16)

How Jesus' words must have shocked Peter, John, and all the disciples gathered at the last supper. Had they not left everything—their jobs, their homes, even their families—to follow Jesus? In him they had found the purpose for their life. They had begun to believe that he was "the Holy One of God," the one who had "the words of eternal life" (John 6:68-69). They had seen him heal multitudes of people, raise the dead, even calm the raging seas. In his name, they themselves had gone out and healed the sick, expelled demons, and proclaimed the kingdom. Why would Jesus leave when everything was going so well?

Within just a few hours of hearing these words, the disciples experienced their full force; they saw Jesus betrayed by one of his closest friends. He was

arrested, beaten, crucified, and buried. Fear filled them and they fled. And, even though they rejoiced at Jesus' resurrection, they still lacked power and boldness. When he left them again, this time to ascend into heaven, they were once more alone. How would they continue now that Jesus was gone? Where was this Comforter, this Advocate, that he had promised?

Shortly after Jesus' departure, on the Jewish feast of Pentecost, this little band of disciples was gathered together in prayer when it finally happened. God's power came down upon them and filled them (Acts 2:1-4). The promised Holy Spirit had come (John 14:25-26)! The disciples were so filled with joy that some onlookers thought they were drunk (Acts 2:13). But they knew differently. They knew that because of the Spirit's presence within them, their prayer had exploded into a whole new dimension of praise and worship of God (2:11).

They were moved to preach boldly about Jesus' triumph over death (2:36). They performed miracles (3:1-10). They could love everyone—even their persecutors—with the love of God (3:17-21). This Holy Spirit for whom they had waited and prayed transformed ordinary, uneducated disciples into bold servants of the gospel (4:13).

The Spirit's Ongoing Work

While that first Pentecost was a day of remarkable power, scripture makes it clear that the outpouring of the Spirit was not meant to be just a one-time occurrence. Throughout the book of Acts, Luke tells numerous stories of the Spirit's ongoing activity, as if to say that what was begun on the day of Pentecost was simply that—only the beginning (see Acts 8:14-17; 10:44-48; 13:1-3; 16:6-10; 19:1-7; 20:22-23).

Apart from the initial experience of joy and boldness, what does the Spirit do when he enters a person? Throughout his letters, Paul gives us a picture of the powerful work of transformation that the Spirit wants to bring about in all believers. To the Ephesians, he spoke of the Spirit granting us unrestrained access to God (Ephesians 2:18). To the Romans, he spoke about the Spirit pouring out God's love on us and freeing us from sin and death (Romans 5:5; 8:2). He told the Thessalonians that it was the Spirit who gave them their strength in the midst of affliction (1 Thessalonians 1:6). To the Corinthians he spoke of the Spirit revealing the glory of Jesus to human hearts (1 Corinthians 2:9-12; 2 Corinthians 3:18).

Do these wonderful gifts of power and comfort sound like things that naturally occur in our lives? Do they sound like the result of "positive thinking," or of our own limited efforts at overcoming sin and

darkness? Rather, in all these instances, we see God continuously pouring out his power and grace. Only God can deliver us from sin. Only God can give us the strength to love and forgive in difficult situations. Only God can make our hearts burn with love for Jesus. And he has done all these things, and more, through the wonderful gift of his Spirit (see *Catechism of the Catholic Church*, 733-736).

Fire, Wind, Water

Just as it happened with the first disciples, so too for us, the coming of the Spirit is bound to shake up our lives. Many of the images scripture uses to describe the Holy Spirit evoke a sense of power—often a power beyond our control. The Spirit is both a fire that burns (Sirach 48:1; Matthew 3:11; CCC, 696) and a wind that blows like the breath of God (John 3:8-9; CCC, 691). The Spirit is the "fin-

"finger of God" that drives out the evil one and imprints God's word on human hearts (Luke 11:20; 2 Corinthians 3:3; CCC, 700). He is the "water of life" that floods into our lives at baptism and that continues to flow, inviting us to be caught up in his current (John 7:37-39; 1 Corinthians 12:13; CCC, 694).

The Spirit is fire, water, and wind. All these images speak of God's desire—and his power—to release us from sin and fill us with his life and love. When he was on the earth, Jesus prayed: "I came to cast fire upon the earth; and would that it were already kindled!" (Luke 12:49). How Jesus desired to reconcile us with the Father and so open the way for the Spirit to fill our hearts! Without his death and resurrection, there could be no Pentecost; there could be no body of Christ; there could be no indwelling Spirit. Prior to Jesus' coming, the Spirit was at work, hovering over creation, inspir-

ing various individuals, and advancing God's purposes for his people. But now, because of Jesus, the Spirit has come to transform the world as he transforms all our lives.

The Spirit In Our Hearts Today

As we are filled ever more deeply with the Spirit, we become more confident in God's abundant love for us and his presence within us. Above all the other ways in which scripture defines the Spirit, the primary definition is that the Holy Spirit is the love of God coming to dwell in our hearts (Romans 5:5; 1 John 4:7-13). The Spirit is the all-consuming love between the Father and the Son, and this is the love that God pours into us, transforming us into beloved sons and daughters. This is the love that brought forth creation at the beginning of time. And it is the same love that later burst forth

and transformed God's people—one by one—into a new creation.

Centuries before Jesus was born, the prophet Jeremiah foretold a new covenant that God would make with his people, a covenant not written on stone tablets, but on human hearts: "I will put my law within them, and I will write it upon their hearts . . . they shall all know me, from the least of them to the greatest, says the LORD" (Jeremiah 31:33-34). Jeremiah's prophecy is fulfilled as we experience—both individually and together as one people in Christ—the power of the Spirit in our hearts. Jesus inaugurated this new covenant when he shed his blood for us. Today, we can experience the Spirit's power to free us from sin, heal our wounds, fill us with God's love, and reveal Jesus to us.

As we approach the day of Pentecost, there are some very practical ways by which we can open ourselves to experience the Spirit's power. Every

day we can ask the Spirit to speak to us and teach us as we pray (John 14:26). We can hear his voice! We can also beg the Spirit to fall with greater power upon everyone: "Come, Holy Spirit, and renew the face of the earth!" (see Psalm 104:30).

Throughout the day, we can try to be aware of the Spirit's presence in our hearts. Call upon him and talk to him. Ask him for strength and peace in difficult situations. Be confident that he does dwell within you (John 14:16-17). When you recognize sin in your life, know that this is the work of the Spirit in you, inviting you to greater freedom, seeking to make you more like Jesus (John 16:8).

Every evening as you get ready to go to bed, spend a few minutes talking to the Spirit, asking him to give you the peace of Christ and to protect you and everyone around you. Thank him for the ways he has worked with you during the day, and ask him to soften your heart even more tomor-

row—ministering God's presence to you in an even deeper way.

"Come, Holy Spirit, and shine the light of God into our hearts. Let your fire purify us of sin and warm our hearts. Let your wind blow the old life away and breathe God's presence into us. Let your rain fall upon us to wash us clean and refresh our spirits. Come, O Spirit, and reveal the glory of Jesus to your people!"

I Will Never Leave You

God is present to us in many ways—in the beauty of creation, in those around us, in our own hearts, and in his church. And yet, at the same time, we can often feel as if we're not in touch with him. The whole thought of experiencing God can seem mysterious and even contradictory to us. How can we love a God who is so far above us that we can't see him or touch him? The good news is that God is a Person who wants us to know him. So much did he want us to be with him that he gave us his only Son so that we could

be reconciled to him and share our lives with him. In Christ, our sin has been forgiven, and through the outpouring of his Spirit, we can now know God as a loving, faithful Father.

In this chapter, we explore some of the ways God comes to meet us in our day-to-day lives. By the power of the Spirit, he lives within us. He speaks his words of life to us in scripture, and we know his presence when we gather with other Christians. In a special way, he invites us to see him in the poor and outcast. In all these ways, we have wonderful opportunities to experience the mercy and power of our God.

As we meet the Lord in these ways, our hearts will slowly be changed by his love. We will find ourselves growing closer to God, more confident in his love for us. We will be moved to share that love with others. We will find ourselves praying "Come, Lord Jesus" more frequently and with more hope

and expectation. Whenever you see these things happening in you, be encouraged: God is at work in you, fulfilling his promises and making his presence known to you more deeply.

Jesus Alive In Us

We saw in the last chapter that God poured out his Spirit in order to fill us with the presence and power of Jesus. St. Paul wrote: "God's love has been poured into our hearts through the Holy Spirit which has been given to us" (Romans 5:5). The Holy Spirit is inside of you. He wants to unite you to Jesus, making you a beloved son or daughter of God (Romans 8:15-16; CCC, 684). In the days to come, pray to the Spirit; ask him to reveal Jesus to you. Ask him to make Jesus so real to you that you can confidently say you know Jesus Christ (see John 17:3).

Every day, we face ups and downs, and God invites us to offer every situation, every moment, even every failure, to him. Talk to him as you go about your day. Tell him about your thoughts, feelings, and desires, your responsibilities and temptations. Never forget how much God loves you; ask him to be with you and to reassure you of his love, especially in times of difficulty. He is in your heart right now, a generous Father inviting you to know his presence. Never be ashamed to come to him; he is never ashamed of you (Hebrews 2:11). He offered up his Son to bring you into his presence. He is always ready to strengthen and encourage you as you turn to him.

The Scriptures Speak To Our Hearts

Imagine what it must have been like for the two disciples on the road to Emmaus when Jesus—

unrecognizable though he was—explained the scriptures to them (Luke 24:27-33). As they walked along with Jesus and listened to him, their hearts began to burn within them. The tragedy of Jesus' crucifixion had left them desolate, feeling abandoned and without hope. But now, as Jesus opened God's word for them, their sadness and confusion gave way to great joy and expectation. They weren't abandoned after all. Everything they thought had been lost was now restored—and with even greater promise. God was true to his word. He could be trusted.

God wants us to treasure his word because the Spirit is present in scripture in a special way, unveiling the truth about who God is and who we are in him. Whenever we read scripture with open hearts we can experience Jesus' presence and receive the wisdom and direction we need for our daily lives. Just like the disciples on the way to

Emmaus, our hearts too can burn with love and hope as we ask Jesus to explain his words to us: "In the sacred books, the Father who is in heaven comes lovingly to meet his children, and talks with them" (Vatican II, Dogmatic Constitution on Divine Revelation, 21).

Where Two or Three Are Gathered

Picture how exciting the conversation between Mary and Elizabeth must have been at the time of the visitation (Luke 1:39-56). How thrilled they must have been as they shared about the angel's messages and the wonderful ways God was at work. Try to imagine the Holy Spirit present with them, rejoicing in their faith and filling them with joy—even moving Elizabeth's child John to leap in the womb.

Jesus told his disciples: "Where two or three are

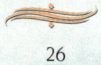

gathered in my name, there am I in the midst of them" (Matthew 18:20). Whenever you are with a fellow believer, you have an immediate opportunity to know God's presence more powerfully. What a blessing it is to talk about scripture, the challenges of living as a Christian in the world, or the dramatic ways God is moving in our times! It's always encouraging to see the Lord working in other people's lives, whether it be in dramatic ways such as healings or conversions, or in the everyday experiences of life. Even when we are just enjoying one another's company and not sharing specifically about the Lord, God is still present, watching over us and blessing us.

In a special way, families can come together in Jesus' name to pray and share their lives. Think about the conversations that Joseph, Mary, and Jesus had at meals, or in their times of prayer together. Pray together as a family, thanking God

for his love, for the beauty of the world around you, and for his plan for your lives. Ask forgiveness of one another and freely forgive each other. Pray for your friends, for your relatives, and for the needy. Tell Jesus that you love him; invite him to join you at meals and in your time together.

"When I Was Naked, You Clothed Me"

Have you ever noticed how easy it is for children to show compassion and help the poor—how simple-hearted and generous they can be? Jesus wants to form a child-like heart in us as well, a heart that recognizes his presence in even the most unloved and outcast of people. He wants us to see the great privilege it is to be able to let Christ, who lives in us, reach out to love these—our precious brothers and sisters. Jesus has made us all ministers of his gospel of peace (Ephesians 6:15). His love

can flow through us to others—even to total strangers—as we learn to practice his presence.

Mother Teresa has repeatedly remarked that the greatest poverty in the Western world is a poverty of love. People are starving for love, even in our own homes. Today, seek to love those whom God puts on your heart. The next time you see a homeless person or someone you know is lonely, recognize Christ and share the love of God through your generosity and through things as simple as a smile and some kind words. Remember Jesus' promise: "Truly, I say to you, as you did it to one of the least of these my brethren, you did it to me" (Matthew 25:40).

In the School of Christ

Right now, as God pours out his Spirit in a powerful way, resolve to try to seek Jesus in every situation and every moment. He is in you; he will

never leave you. Jesus promised to be with you until the end of time (Matthew 28:20). Every hour can be filled with his presence. All we have to do is continue to practice being with him. Remember that this is a learning process, and that God is a patient teacher. We are in the school of Christ every day, and all the lessons work together to produce in us a deeper awareness of God's presence. We can all take encouragement from the words of scripture:

> I am sure that neither death, nor life, nor angels, nor principalities, nor things present, nor things to come, nor powers, nor height, nor depth, nor anything else in all creation, will be able to separate us from the love of God in Christ Jesus our Lord. (Romans 8:38-39)

God Is Truly In Our Hearts

By Brother Lawrence of the Resurrection

The most necessary practice in the spiritual life is the presence of God, that is to take delight in and become accustomed to his divine company, speaking humbly and talking lovingly with him at all times, at every moment without rule or system and especially in times of temptation, suffering, spiritual aridity, disgust and even of unfaithfulness and sin. . . .

Since you know God is with you in all your actions, that he is in the deepest recesses of your soul, why not, from time to time, leave off your external activities and even your spoken prayers to adore him inwardly, to praise him, to petition him, to offer him your heart and to give him thanks?

What can be more agreeable to God than to withdraw many times a day from the things of man to retire into ourselves and adore him interiorly? These interior retreats to God gradually free us by destroying that self-love which can exist only among our fellow human beings . . . . All these acts of adoration should be made by faith, knowing that God is truly in our hearts.

Taken from the writings of Brother Lawrence,
The Practice of the Presence of God.

Bread for Our Journey

As we have already seen, God has made his presence and power available to us in many different ways. At baptism, God comes to dwell in our hearts through his Holy Spirit. As we grow and learn to yield to the Spirit, our experience of God and his presence grows and deepens as well. We begin to hear him speak to us in scripture. We taste his presence when we gather with other Christians. We meet him as we care for the poor and needy around us.

In addition to these ways, scripture speaks of yet

another avenue, an extraordinary way in which Jesus can transform us with his presence—his body and blood in the Eucharist. In this chapter, we look at the life that is available to us in the Eucharist and reflect on the attitude of heart that can open us up to all the blessings God wants to pour out through this sacrament.

Bread in the Desert

Jesus' presence in the Eucharist is prefigured in the story of God feeding the Israelites with manna in the desert (Exodus 16-20). As they traveled day after day through the Sinai desert on their way to the promised land, many of the Israelites began to feel that their journey was a curse from God. They blamed Moses for leading them into such desolation: "Would that we had died by the hand of the LORD in the land of Egypt . . . for you have brought us out into this wilderness to kill this whole assembly with hunger" (Exodus 16:3). How quickly they forgot that they had been slaves in Egypt, robbed of dignity and oppressed with hard labor. They even lost sight of the fact that Pharaoh had ordered the murder of their children in an effort to control their numbers (Exodus 1:11-16).

In the midst of these challenges, the journey in the desert was, in fact, a time of great blessing for the Israelites. God revealed his presence to them on Mount Sinai—something that no other nation had experienced (Exodus 19:16-25; Psalm 147:19-20). He was continually with them, guiding them with a cloud during the day and a pillar of fire at night (Exodus 40:36-38). Scripture tells us that even the smallest details were cared for: Their shoes and clothing didn't wear out during their entire forty-year journey (Deuteronomy 29:5). When they cried out in thirst, God gave them water from a rock (Exodus 17:5-8). When they were hungry, he fed them with manna and quail (Exodus 16:13-15). God always heard their prayers and cared for them, even as he sought to form them as his covenanted people.

Of all these signs, the miracle of the manna especially showed God's love for his people—his desire to provide for them every day of their lives. Every morning, God sent the Israelites only enough manna to last one day (Exodus 16:16-19). He didn't want them to collect more than a day's needs, and when some tried to store some away for the next day, it became wormy and spoiled (16:20). God was displeased by this, because his people were trying to find a way to avoid having to depend on him on a continuing basis. They didn't trust him to be faithful to his promise to care for their needs, but he wanted to be their sole support.

The Bread of Life

This story of the manna in the desert provides the background for the section of John's Gospel that describes Jesus as the bread of life (John 6:1-71). The day after Jesus had multiplied the loaves and fishes, the same crowd that had witnessed this miracle went looking for Jesus (6:22-24). When they found him, Jesus told them: "Do not labor for the food which perishes but for the food which endures to eternal life, which the Son of man will give to you" (6:27). Knowing that the crowd was caught up with the "perishable"—the bread and the miracles that Jesus was performing—Jesus sought to turn their eyes toward the "imperishable"—the mercy of God and his loving presence (see CCC, 547-549).

The people, struggling to understand Jesus' words, asked him: "What must we do, to be doing the works of God?" (John 6:28). Jesus replied that the "work of God" was to believe in him (6:29). Jesus was interested in something deeper than signs and wonders; he wanted their trust and faith. Faith seeks God's presence. Those with faith place their lives in Jesus' hands every day, expecting to experience something more than their eyes can see.

This is the kind of faith that can experience Jesus in the Eucharist. Both in the Eucharist and in everyday life, Jesus wants to be the source of our strength and wisdom, our hope and our courage. Every day, he wants to guide us and provide for us, just as he did for the Israelites in the desert. Every day, he longs for us to turn to him and receive him—Jesus, the bread of life—into our hearts.

Jesus' listeners began to murmur and grumble at his words, just as the Israelites did in the desert. His invitation to them to receive the bread of life distressed them and challenged their faith, to the point that most of them walked away (John 6:66; CCC, 1336). Yet the twelve—Jesus' closest disciples—stayed with him. Peter told Jesus: "Lord, to whom shall we go? You have the words of eternal life" (John 6:68). Their hearts had been touched; they knew that only Jesus could provide for their needs. They recognized that Jesus was the true bread of life, and they wanted to be fed by him every day.

A Heart Burning with Desire

From the earliest days of his life, it was recognized that Jesus would be "a sign that is spoken against" (Luke 2:34)—someone who would not be easily accepted. Many people heard Jesus teach and saw him perform miracles. News of his power swept through Galilee and Judea, and he began to attract large crowds (Mark 1:32; John 12:12-18).

Some—like Zacchaeus (Luke 19:1-10) and Matthew (Matthew 9:9-13)—were transformed when they met Jesus. Some—like Peter (Luke 5:2-8) and the sinful woman (Luke 7:36-50)—were brought to their knees in repentance and worship. Still others heard Jesus and walked away, their lives hardly changed at all (John 6:60-65). How Jesus suffered over those who could not understand that God was reaching out from heaven to touch them (Matthew 23:37-39)!

At the last supper, Jesus told his disciples: "I have earnestly desired to eat this passover with you before I suffer" (Luke 22:15). His heart burned with such love that he continued resolutely toward Calvary, even though he knew what awaited him. Jesus considered the cross a worthy price to pay if it meant rescuing us from sin and reuniting us with our Father.

Even today, Jesus' heart continues to burn with

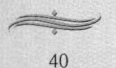

desire for us. As we receive the body and blood of Jesus in the Eucharist, God's burning love is made available to us, just as it was made available to Peter and the others. Jesus wants to heal and transform us, to fill us with his presence. Yet, it is possible that we too could come into his presence and still walk away unchanged.

Jesus' invitation to eat his body and drink his blood should shake us up and challenge us. John's account gives two options as we come to receive the Eucharist. We can receive Jesus' presence and pray like Peter: "You are the Holy One of God" (John 6:69), or we can walk away unchanged (6:60). As we come to the table of the Lord, let us fix our eyes and hearts on Jesus. As we are united with him in a living and humble faith, he has promised that we will never hunger or thirst. Just as he fed the Israelites and took care of their every need, the Father himself will care for us as we place our lives in his hands.

"O Lord, help us to welcome the Holy Spirit deeper into our hearts. Enable us to open our hearts to Jesus as he comes to us in the Eucharist. Fill us with your love and your power so that we may be a pleasing dwelling place for the Lord. Spirit, create in us a longing for Jesus' table which he so much wants to share with us."

One With the Lord

"The Eucharist . . . re-presents (makes present) the sacrifice of the cross, because it is its memorial and because it applies its fruit." (*Catechism of the Catholic Church*, 1366)

When we gather to celebrate the Eucharist, the Spirit is present in a special way, offering us a deeper share in Jesus' death and resurrection. St. Paul wrote: "As often as you eat this bread and drink the cup, you proclaim the Lord's death until he comes" (1 Corinthians 11:26), pointing to the union with Jesus that is available to us in the Eucharist. Just as we were joined to Jesus in his death and resurrection at baptism (Romans 6:1-11), now when-

and humility, we can experience ever more deeply the truth that we are crucified with Jesus, and that he now lives in us (Galatians 2:20). As we allow the cross of Christ to free us more completely from sin and bondage, we will experience the power of his Spirit transforming us into Jesus' image.

Jesus, Bread From Heaven

Jesus is our true bread as we journey through life. The following invocations are taken from the Litany for Holy Communion, a prayer that reflects the precious gift of Jesus in the Eucharist.

Jesus, living Bread which came down from heaven, have mercy on us.

Jesus, Bread from heaven giving life to the world, have mercy on us.

Jesus, hidden God and Savior, have mercy on us.

Jesus, who has loved us with an everlasting love, have mercy on us.

Jesus, whose delights are to be with your children, have mercy on us.

Jesus, who has given your flesh for the life of the world, have mercy on us.

Jesus, who invites all to come to you, have mercy on us.

Jesus, who promises eternal life to those who receive you, have mercy on us.

Jesus, who with desire desires to eat this Pasch with us, have mercy on us.

Jesus, ever ready to receive and welcome us, have mercy on us.

Jesus, who stands at our door knocking, have mercy on us.

Jesus, who has said that if we will open the door to you, you will come in and eat with us, have mercy on us.

Jesus, who receives us into you arms and blesses us with the little children, have mercy on us.

Jesus, who invites us to sit at your feet with Mary Magdalen, have mercy on us.

Jesus, who has not left us orphans, have mercy on us.

Most dear Sacrament,

Sacrament of love,

Sacrament of sweetness,

Life-giving Sacrament,

Sacrament of strength,

My God and my all.